W9-BGU-807

Snakes!

Melissa Stewart

Washington, D.C.

For Rubin
—M.S.

Published by the National Geographic Society, Washington, D.C. 20036

Library of Congress Cataloging-in-Publication Data
Stewart, Melissa.
Snakes! / by Melissa Stewart.
p. cm.
ISBN 978-1-4263-0428-6 (pbk. : alk. paper) — ISBN 978-1-4263-0429-3 (hardcover : alk. paper)
1. Snakes—Juvenile literature. I. Title.
QL666.06S87 2009
597.96—dc22
2008047001

Printed in the United States of America

Cover: © Heidi & Hans-Jurgen Koch/drr.net; 1: © Martin Harvey/DRK Photo; 2, 20-21, 25 (middle), 32 (bottom, left): © Digital Vision; 4-5: © Michael D. Kern/Nature Picture Library; 6-7: © Jerry Young/Dorling Kindersley/DK Images; 7 (top): © Colin Keates/Dorling Kindersley/Getty Images; 8, 9, 32 (top, right): © Norbert Rosing/National Geographic/Getty Images; 10: © DeAgostini Picture Library/Getty Images; 11 (top): © Joe & Mary Ann McDonald/ Getty Images; 11 (bottom, left): © Anthony Bannister/Gallo Images/Getty Images; 11 (bottom, right), 27 (bottom), 32 (middle, left): © Michael & Patricia Fogden/Corbis; 12 (top): © Lowell Georgia/Corbis; 12 (bottom): © Michael & Patricia Fogden/Minden Pictures/National Geographic Stock; 13: © Frank Lane Picture Agency/Corbis; 14 (top), 32 (top, left): © Bianca Lavies/National Geographic/Getty Images; 14-15: © Joe McDonald/Corbis; 16, 25 (top), 32 (bottom, right): © Ashok Captain/ephotocorp/Alamy; 17 (top, left): © Image Source/Corbis; 17 (top, right): © Paul Chesley/Stone/Getty Images; 17 (bottom): © Dwayne Brown/Brownstock Inc./Alamy; 18: © Francois Savigny/ Minden Pictures; 18-19 (bottom): © Tony Phelps/Nature Picture Library; 19 (top): © Dr. George Gornacz/Science Photo Library; 19 (bottom, right): © S. Blair Hedges, Ph.D., Penn. State; 22 (top, left): © Frans Lemmens/zefa/Corbis; 22 (top, right), 23 (top, right): © Michael & Patricia Fogden/Minden Pictures; 22-23 (background): © Darrell Gulin/Corbis; 23 (top, left), 31 (top): © Shutterstock; 24: © Dorling Kindersley/Getty Images; 25 (bottom): © Thomas C. Brennan; 26: © Stephen Dalton/Minden Pictures; 27 (top): © Mark Moffett/ Minden Pictures/National Geographic Stock; 28, 32 (middle, right): © Theo Allofs/Corbis; 29 (top): © Oliver Strewe/Stone/Getty Images; 29 (bottom): © Werner Bollmann/Photolibrary/Getty Images; 30: © John & Lisa Merrill/Photodisc/Getty Images; 31 (bottom): © A&J Visage/Alamy.

Table of Contents

It's a Snake!

What is long and round,
and slides on the ground?

What can be fat or thin,
and has dry, scaly skin?

AMAZON TREE BOA

What has a tongue that flicks,
and eyes that can't blink?

For goodness sake . . .

. . . it's a snake!

A snake is a reptile. Lizards, turtles, and crocodiles are reptiles, too.

All reptiles have tough scales. A snake has stretchy skin between its scales.

A reptile's body is always the same temperature as the air around it. To warm up, a snake lies in the sun. To cool down, a snake moves into the shade.

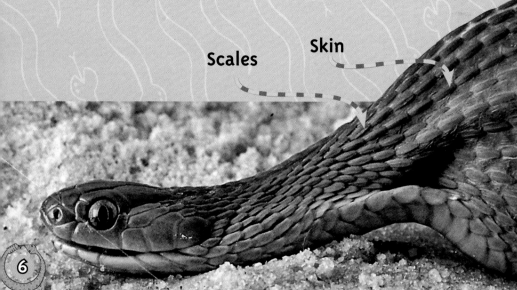

Skin

Scales

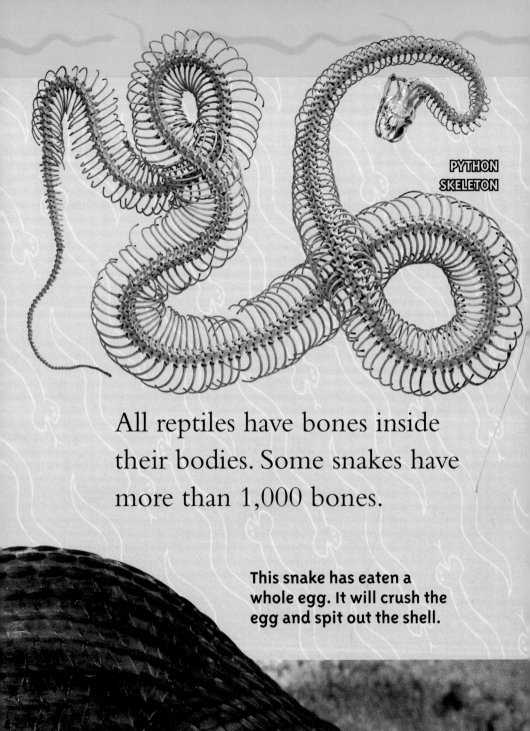

PYTHON
SKELETON

All reptiles have bones inside
their bodies. Some snakes have
more than 1,000 bones.

This snake has eaten a
whole egg. It will crush the
egg and spit out the shell.

EGG SNAKE

Snakes
All Around

W🔘rds-s-s

HIBERNATE: In winter, some animals have trouble finding food. To save energy, their bodies slow down. The animals rest in a safe place.

Snakes live in fields and forests.
They live in deserts and oceans too.
They even live in city parks. Snakes
can live almost anywhere.

Most snakes live in warm places.
They stay active all year long.

Some snakes live in cool places.
In the winter, they hibernate. Most
snakes hibernate alone. Some snakes
hibernate in large groups.

Each winter,
thousands of
garter snakes
hibernate together
in southern Canada.

In the spring the
garters slither out
of their warm dens.

Snakes and More Snakes

INDIAN COBRA WITH EGGS

In warm places, mother snakes usually lay eggs. Then they slither away. They do not take care of the eggs.

Most snakes lay 20 or 30 eggs.
Large pythons may lay up to 100 eggs.

After a few weeks, the eggs hatch.
The young snakes look just like
their parents.

BURMESE PYTHONS HATCHING

GREEN MAMBA
HATCHING

CORAL SNAKE HATCHING

YOUNG DIAMONDBACK RATTLER

In cool places, snakes usually grow inside their mother's body. A mother snake lies in the sun to keep the little snakes warm.

EYELASH VIPER WITH JUST-BORN YOUNG

Q: What do you get when you cross a young bird with a puff adder?

A: A chick who is good at math.

PUFF ADDER WITH SOME OF HER YOUNG

Most mother snakes give birth to between 5 and 20 little snakes. A puff adder can give birth to more than 150 snakes at once. Imagine what it would feel like to have all those tiny wigglers inside your body!

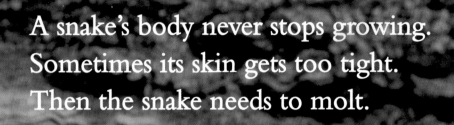

A snake's body never stops growing. Sometimes its skin gets too tight. Then the snake needs to molt.

TIMBER RATTLESNAKE

EGYPTIAN BANDED COBRA

The snake rubs its head
against a rock. Its skin splits open.
Then the snake crawls forward.
Its skin can peel off in one long piece.
It's like taking off a sock.

Most snakes molt
3 or 4 times a year.

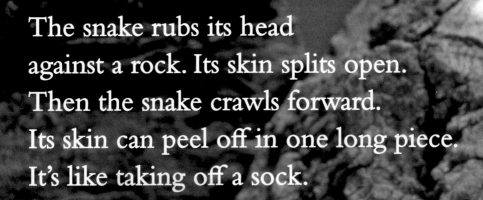

Words-s-s

MOLT: When animals molt, they lose their old skin, fur, or feathers. New skin is underneath.

On the Move

Most animals have legs and feet. But not a snake. Scutes help a snake move forward.

Scute

Words-s-s

SCUTES: The wide scales on the belly of a snake.

PIT VIPER

Q What did the pit viper say as it slithered around the rat snake?

A *Ex-scutes-me.*

A python crawls forward in a straight line. Its belly muscles push its scutes against the ground.

Scutes can't grip desert sand. A sidewinding adder has to throw its body sideways to move forward.

PYTHON

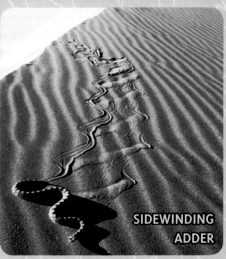

SIDEWINDING ADDER

A garter snake curves its body back and forth. Its scutes push against grass and rocks.

GARTER SNAKE

Super Snakes

Heaviest

GREEN ANACONDA
A green anaconda can weigh up to 550 pounds. That's as much as a lion!

There are about 2,700 different kinds of snakes.

Most Poisonous

BEAKED SEA SNAKE
This deadly snake lives in shallow areas of the Indian Ocean. It can stay underwater for up to 5 hours.

Fastest

BLACK MAMBA
A black mamba can travel up to 12 miles per hour. That's twice as fast as most people can run.

Smallest

LESSER ANTILLEAN THREAD SNAKE
The lesser Antillean thread snake was discovered in 2001.

Snake Senses

Snakes use their senses to escape from danger. Senses also help snakes hunt for food.

Snakes with round pupils hunt during the day. Snakes with long, thin pupils hunt at night.

Some snakes smell with their noses. But all snakes smell with their tongues. Their tongues are split at the tip. This helps them know if they should go left or right.

A snake's ears are deep inside its head. Sound travels through a snake's bones to its ears.

Some snakes have heat pits. They can sense the body heat of other animals. Heat pits help snakes hunt at night.

Nostril

Heat pit

Pupil

Words-s-s

PUPIL: The dark area at the center of the eye. It lets light into the eye.

ARUBA RATTLESNAKE

Where's the Snake?

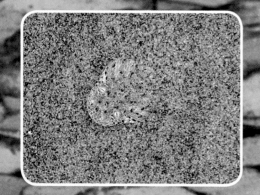

GARTER SNAKE IN WATER

Most snakes are hard to see.
They blend in with their
surroundings.

Can you spot the snakes in these pictures?

Hiding helps
snakes stay safe
from predators.
Hiding also helps
snakes catch prey.

W🔵rds-s-s

PREDATORS:
Animals that eat
other animals.

PREY:
Animals that are
eaten by other
animals.

23

There's the Snake!

Some snakes do not hide from predators. They have other ways of staying safe.

Some snakes play dead when an enemy gets too close.

GRASS SNAKE

Q If a snake went to school, what would its favorite class be?

A Hiss-tory

A spitting cobra sprays its predators' eyes with poisonous spit.

A coral snake is full of poison. Its bright colors warn predators to stay away.

Some snakes hiss at predators. Others rattle their tails. A western hooked-nose snake pushes air out of its back end. The farting sound travels up to six feet.

25

Snake Snacks

Most snakes eat about 30 meals a year. Snakes catch prey with their sharp teeth.

Many snakes have more than 200 teeth. If a snake loses a tooth, a new one quickly grows in.

Cobras, vipers, and pit vipers have large teeth. They are called fangs.

PUFF ADDER VIPER

TAIWAN HABU VIPER

Poison flows through holes in a snake's fangs. Some poisons stop prey from moving. Other poisons kill the prey.

EYELASH VIPER STRIKING AT HUMMINGBIRD

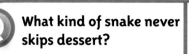

Most snakes catch small animals. They eat mice, frogs, fish, and birds. These snakes eat their prey live.

GREEN TREE SNAKE

They stretch their mouths wide open. Then they swallow the animal headfirst.

Pythons, boas, and rat snakes can eat large animals. They coil their thick bodies around their prey. Then they squeeze it to death. A large python can easily kill an antelope.

A CARPET SNAKE PUTTING THE SQUEEZE ON A LIZARD

AFRICAN ROCK PYTHON

Snake Pets

Most snakes are not dangerous to humans. Snakes eat mice, rats, and insects that we do not want in our homes or eating our crops. Snakes are an important part of our world.

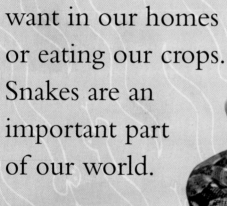

BOA CONSTRICTOR

Some people like snakes so much that they keep them as pets. Did you know snakes are ticklish? And they are cool and dry and soft. There is nothing else quite like a snake!

BOA CONSTRICTOR

RETICULATED PYTHON

MOLT
When animals molt, they lose their old skin, fur, or feathers. New skin is underneath.

HIBERNATE
Some animals rest during the winter. They slow their bodies down to save energy.

PREDATORS
Animals that eat other animals.

PREY
Animals that are eaten by other animals.

PUPIL
The dark area at the center of the eye. It lets light into the eye.

SCUTES
Scutes are the wide scales on the belly of a snake.